The Bridge That Carries the Road

The Bridge
That Carries the Road

Lynn Davies

Brick Books

CANADIAN CATALOGUING IN PUBLICATION DATA

Davies, Lynn, 1954–
  The bridge that carries the road

Poems.

ISBN 1-894078-01-2

I. Title.

PS8557.A81967B74 1999   C811'.54   C99-930431-3
PR9199.3.D38B74 1999

We acknowledge the support of the Canada Council for the Arts
for our publishing programme. The support of the Ontario Arts
Council is also gratefully acknowledged.

Cover art: *Paper Crossing the Meeting of Waters: Stream and Sea*,
Newfoundland 1982, photo/landwork by Marlene Creates,
(CARfac©Collective). Collection: The Canada Council Art Bank.

Typeset in Ehrhardt.
The stock is acid-free Zephyr Antique laid.
Printed and bound by The Porcupine's Quill Inc.

Brick Books
431 Boler Road, Box 20081
London, Ontario, N6K 4G6

brick.books@sympatico.ca

This book is for
John
Josie and Patrick

You will still sleep many hours
here on the beach,
and one clear morning you will find
your boat tied to another shore.

– Antonio Machado

Contents

The Onion Mountains

My Silent Days

I met my cowboy on a car ferry sailing to Newfoundland. Heeled boots, bright Stetson all the way from Kamloops, B.C., distant land back then. On the ferry deck a wild east wind blew my poncho to pieces, furious speech I was grateful for. Those were my silent days when talking to a man was picking at an icefield with a broken nailfile while looking the other way. He was gesture, rough hands but warm, rock falling past me to rattle below. On Signal Hill's cliff he flung his watch into the air, a perfect ticking arc for the great blue waiting below us. All time gone in the flex of an arm and was I impressed until he told me he had another watch like it back home. No rain those days walking old streets and before he left he cried. On a ship bound for Portugal, months later a postcard from Iceland. I've been through his country now, hills rolling to rise into more hills, too dry for trees.

In the Beginning

In the beginning was the highway. Knitting needles and variegated
brown-yellow wool in my pack, distance on folded paper.

Twice you found me waiting by the road. I dreamed sock but knit a hole
in the tire. So many wildflowers I couldn't name. Our silence.

Like a leaf, the canoe. Unravelled early fall up a lake. Dusk-
foolish moose and her calf, the white lights fluid above us.

Innocent, we cast off into waves pouring walls on the beach.
Wind culled paddling, hummocky moss dead end. The map forgot us.

By the orange spotted touch-me-not. Or jewelweed. We drove south
through the badlands. When I cut the yarn, my sock fit a giant.

What Came Before Me

When we beached the canoe we shed our clothes
to walk the white sand beside the green lake.
We heard feathers part air and I remember
a beaver wake at dusk and geese flying south
through the night. We rose to a wild
morning necklace of wolf tracks. To think
we might have felt their warm breath swell our tent
walls like sails grateful to Aeolus.

                    Ten years later
I open the front door to new snow,
see cat prints flee light like beads
floating free of fine line. I turn to tell you
what came before me but my words fall
to the evening news where you seek
what I fear most.

Songs for Gravity

1

In the window
we found twenty-three moths resting
their wings. Translucent, letting morning light in.
Scallop-edged wings. Cream fringe,
    a scarf torn apart by the night.

2

Bright marigolds lift
their blooms to late afternoon
sun's lessons in light.

3

Only a gray house at the end of a lane,
its windows and doors boarded up and blind
to the slow drift and rise
of dandelion seeds. No birds dip
      through noon here.
Our children climb an old tree,
clumps of moss pelt the ground
    scare a mouse in long grass.

4

How old man's beard
hangs lace-down from trees.
Holds water like berries
        left by the fog
    to break on the ground.

5

A sea-rock bowl
full of still water.
Until my son's rubber boot

        plunged in
    makes a river
            rise to follow
    a rock seam's path
        to the sand.

6

In spring the Solomon's seal pokes through
soil first. Its leaves will point
to where it came from, where it will go,
and other springs to come. Only the tiny
flowers hidden along the
weighted stems swing white,
have time for fragrance
    in the cool evening.

7

Remember the house
at the edge of the field, the wild
grass yielding
to deep green hills. Not all
twenty-three moths
flew away.

8

Perched on a feeder at the end
of a rope tied to old eaves troughing,
you fill a belly
white as Indian pipe.
Oh little bird
what silence do you know
at night when snowflakes
falling under a streetlight
send their shadows ahead,
black holes to fall into.

Some of Us Leave in the Way We Came

Some of us leave in the way we came
through time in the womb. The sun declines
so shadow can rise quiet as night
up the mountain. We see darkness coming,
watch the slow subtraction of hair and bone,
see memory drift like first flakes of snow
brushing evergreens. But what of those
who leave in the way a mountain lets go
a broad slope of creature, tree and stone
in the night? Consider the silence
after the slide, the valley altered,
and remember the lilies
scattering light
on heaps of old rubble.

Cape Enrage

Only a picture from a blue tin box.
                                    The day
we shared lunch on a blanket over stones, my mother
pouring from a thermos, steam curling like smoke,
the cocoa dark as the Fundy tide relinquishing the flats,
        exposed mud shiny as a giant's mirror.
My footprints trekking through clouds and sky,
searching for the spot where the tide turns.

                                    In the picture
I wear the moss green jacket my mother sewed for me.
Hold my father's hand under a cliff, in the cave
he told me never dried out between tides.
Then the slow drive down a dirt road so narrow
            we had to shut windows to keep out the leaves,
            frantic as trapped insects against the glass.
Onto the lined, somnolent pavement
leading inland to bed where I lay thinking
of that cave full of ocean,
all entrance gone.

When I Drive Down Highways

When I drive down highways by ditches flowing in milkweed
bright with goldenrod, I hold words to my ears
hear them over the wind whistling past glass and steel
and in the dark behind my eyes I spread boughs,
lie down to wait for the light sound emanates
before it settles into syllable, rises into word
like a trout climbing air for flies. I search
those signs by the side of the road claiming rivers,
naming towns, spreading promises of food cooked fast,
beds made, full tanks of gas, and I wrap green
exits round my shoulders, hold east under my tongue,
see letters part to flick of fin pulling away.

Solomon's Seal

Something needs to be said about the Solomon's seal
in my garden. How the yellow leaves
       hint at the tarnish to come.

Valiant in late October, this fine gold inlay
against a fence, a garage, over grass still thick and green.
       A burnished cup, old as amber.

One of the first to push above ground in spring.
Now a thin-limbed forest falling in golden angles.
Even the spiders have rolled up their webs
       like tents, and gone.

Chestnuts

In the fall, there are chestnuts, bald and secret with grain. We spread them to dry on the table under the oak tree in the back yard. As leaves fall through days tired of light, the mahogany heads shrink. Become mottled with thought, age in ridges and mounds. So unlike the heads I saw in a museum case when a child. Black hair still attached, twisted round silver mounting pins. Their faces sullen and muddy, their eyelids heavy as oilcloth. I was ravenous for details. Who ate the bodies to leave the heads? Did kids like me swing those heads on sticks? Even my taxidermist uncle, sorting glass eyes into coffee tins, grew tired of my questions. Now, the chestnuts drying under the tree grow fetal brows and cheekbones. Veins trickle to the surface. I wait for the eyes to open.

Party Line

At night our cat sits on my desk, staring at the wounds left by men in daylight. In yellow coats and rubber boots, they climbed the maple tree to saw off the branches curling twig fingers down power lines. For two days those stumps bled sap, finally healed honey-gold under the sun. The cat stares, because those foreshortened limbs seem to stare back. When I rise to a child's night cry, I look out the window too. Under the streetlight, those stumps are three full moon faces longing for orbit. When my ears begin to crackle with voices travelling a faulty line in a storm, the cat stands up. If we waited long enough, would dark singing enter the room, lead us down tunnels to the dreams of strangers, invite us in to play? How glad I am for mornings when the boats call from the harbour, and we lie together guessing the weight of fog on our house, and on the earth turning green again.

Six Angels in Clay

Six angels made from clay hang in our window. My daughter suspended them with strands of coloured yarn tied to a popsicle stick. She didn't notice the slight angle of ascension she gave them. A hint of rising over the forsythia, bush burning in the dusk, cool lemon flames, perhaps fragrant. I sit inside, the world too shiny with wet in March. If my bones, so light anyway, could empty to hold long tunnels for flight, then the glass would part for me as water parts for others. I hear the angels, even when they're not moving. They murmur, the way clay does, still of the earth.

Sight

Deepest eyes
my infant's eyes.
Two black holes
floating new space.
See her pupils
distil the light
of this hard world,
stare unflinchingly.
My skin is peeling,
my lips blistering, hair
falling out, she searches me
as if I'm newborn.

Time Change

The night we set the clocks back,
we walked beside a black pond
pinned with stars I thought
were the frozen stares
of prehistoric, one-eyed fish.

Riding on her father's shoulders,
my daughter arched
her neck to the stars
in the sky for the first time
and asked

could we pick them?

These nights
I lie in bed
and see only
the spaces
between things.

The Flamingo

On the thirteenth day of rain my three year old daughter
follows me into a kitchen the size of a closet
to ask for a piece of flamingo. A piece of what?
She repeats her request for a piece of flamingo please,

pointing to the mango in the bowl in the window.
In that moment I see beyond car headlights
in the parking lot at noon. Haul home
late at night my net of long legs, limp neck,

and my days blossom before me. I sauté
flamingo steaks in cinnamon and red peppers,
boil the heart to throw to the beasts
that followed me home. Hang the curved beak

over the back door for good luck. In a dark room
I stack kindling, long legs snapping,
folding neatly as white canes for the blind.
Over the rhubarb not up, I impale broad wings

spread like dusk over dark islands. I poke holes
in hollow bones for my breath, float
soft down in my bath, plait feathers in hair
I could never grow to my waist.

The rest I stuff into bags before questions come
from the neighbours I hear through thin walls,
and when the garbage men descend from the truck
a pink cloud rises on the wind, escapes the bin

and the men throw down their gloves,
strike wild arabesques in steel-toed boots,
reach high for the flesh-hued down.
Ah, what fools we are for some colour

in winter I mutter to my girl
still waiting in the gray kitchen for a
piece of mango ripening in the window
on another day too rainy to play outside.

Friends No Closer to Dar es Salaam

From so far away, and a face black as slate
hot in the sun, he could shriek like a witch
gone mad, spring high as the kitchen window sill
      looking for my daughter: to flap wings
between parked cars, give life to bears, die
once more! They made the world turn crazy
on the tire swing, her hair like grass
blowing gold in a mountain meadow,
his coiled close like dark hornets
      resting on an ebony skull.
The day he left their thin arms
wrapped around each other hid from me
      the ground giving way
before the swing drops to rise
again. That day he speared the oak tree
with his Halloween pitchfork, wept
      on his mother's belly. In the drizzle
the car turned left, was gone. A family
      moving on again, and still
no closer to Dar es Salaam than before.

Today the Roofers Are Out

Today the roofers are out and snow is a memory.
The dark-eyed child sits at her desk,
cannot follow numbers or find words
on a page. If only she could be the dream
of the cartoon whale she's seen swim on TV,
or the appetite of the bobcat her father knows,
skirting what's left of the lake's ice. The lines
of her hand, the lines of the broken pavement in the playground
are kind to her. A roofer choosing a nail
tells her when a spring storm covers the roads,
the birds roost deep in spruce trees,
save their singing for another time. Spring
dries in her like the tar he spreads on the roof.
Even the coltsfoot breaking through gravel hurt her eyes.

When a Child Gets Lost

When a child gets lost in the long grass
only the ghosts of birds underground
      can hear her cries.
And some days the playground becomes
the night highway missing white lines
she will learn to drive down,
or walk beside. It's the undertow
at the ocean's edge I fear. Its power
to pull her small body into water
so deep her eyes will erase me forever.
Yet I remember making houses in the tall grass.
The osprey, leaving its nest high in the elm dying
where the grass goes down to the river,
only the osprey knew where I was,
      wouldn't tell.

Tonight the Violent Wind

(Christmas Eve, 1992)

In the rocking chair, by our tree wearing lights,
carved birds, red sleighs, I listen to John
pound the last minute details into a gift
for our daughter. Our children sleep at last,
while a choir on the radio sings
for the one born in a barn so long ago.
      But yesterday, under trees not far from here,
a trapper found the weather-raked bones of a human being,
all that's left of a teenage girl
who disappeared here last New Year's Day.
                        The papers report
autopsy in progress, foul play suspected.
Residents of the area wonder why she lay
undiscovered for so long, hidden in the grass,
only a stone's throw from the grove of birch trees
where people walk their dogs, stop and have a smoke
all the time. So bleak, the way the road ends
for the young woman leaving home with a backpack
like me, some twenty years ago.
                          Downstairs
he completes his gift: the workbench, fitted
with a vise, two clamps, a handsaw and hammer.
      Tonight the violent wind is a gift,
the way it rips scarlet bows from the house
across the street, enters our home to give me
the smell of old ashes in the bucket by the stove.

Two Corner Stores

Across the road, there was a corner store in the basement of the peeling house. Often my mother sent me to buy a tin of beans or spaghetti, hard to find on the dusty shelves under the dim lights and curled papers studded with flies. Too many children with sticks and names spilled out of that house in the summer to prick tar bubbles on a road that seared our bare feet. Sometimes the oldest girl came to babysit my sister and me. In the darkening house she ordered us under the beds as another summer storm threw cutlery into the sky. We were afraid of the mother, who always carried a child on her big garbage-bag hips, who never smiled but took our pennies for the jawbreakers, the cherrybombs, the sugared mint leaves.

In the summer we went swimming where the river turns salty. One hot afternoon, the whistles cleared the water. What I remember most is the silence of adults gathered to watch the lifeguards cover a body on the beach. Send home, under a gray blanket, the oldest boy from the corner store, only his foot showing.

Soon we had a new store. A beige-sided building next to a field soon to be dug up for another bungalow. A woman sat on a stool, reading a book, waiting to take our money. I could see everything in there, even to the top shelves holding blue boxes of sanitary napkins. I was still wondering what could be more sanitary than the paper dinner napkins wrapped in plastic my mother sent me to buy for summer barbecues. I didn't know then, but I was beginning to understand the price of things, the pool of blood at birth, the bargains made with God.

The Dolphins

When the dolphins leave, they carry their songs deep into the ocean. On the shore, a woman collects stones but cannot name herself. She watches the sun pull darkness from the trees, tries to weave these shadows into a boat. She remembers seeing carved in stone three men sharing a blanket, dreaming of the same angel. Their bed a kind of boat, all they had to do was close their eyes. If she could swim like the dolphins, that too would be an act of faith. The ocean finding her feet sounds like my pencil moving across this page. A sound that rides water eddies off rocks, follows the currents to where the dolphins learned to sing.

When Ships Sail Too Close

When a storm turns the corner, she wonders where to look,
at the raindrops on the window, or the wreckage outside.
Snow resigned to slush, the rain pulling rivers
from driveways, braiding currents down the roads.
The farther she looks, the more she thinks she

might know and understand. How icebergs grow,
and the evolving thoughts of people in cars
stalled in the lakes fed by the rivers. She's heard
that the eyes of old sea captains stay strong,
searching the horizon for lost ships, weather, and land.
One summer she saw the dusky ocean

meet way out there a line of metallic gold so hot
it would ignite any ship that sailed too close.
Now branches take root in the wind,
strain the silent arms holding the ground together.
In the rain-speckled window beside her,
reflections – a lamp, a pillow, two children playing.

Distance

At two in the morning, I think of the animals
who open their eyes, like me, to a train's whistle
finding passage through these mountains.
Each limb of the beech tree outside my window
holds snow the way I carry the sound of your voice.
In these pre-winter days, I watch the mountains
stand up in the same light that wears me down,
clarity taking off like the waxwings
chased by two ravens at the treeline.
Tonight all the passes are closed
and slick with freezing rain. I think of you
listening to the foghorn drone over the ocean
cooling down on the other side of a country
so big in the morning, the sun will find you
three hours before it shines on me here.

Gifts

I walked into town
to buy a gift
for my daughter.

I saw many
polished stones
set in silver

but nothing
that might suggest
the light

I find in her.
Until walking
in late afternoon

three thousand
miles away

from home,
I saw hanging
round her neck

the half moon
stone framed
by the sky.

Grounded

Every year we mimic the stars, rely on lights
strung on trees, on shrubs, and houses,

even basketball hoops. We try to pierce
the longest nights of the year with

filaments in glass bulbs that flicker
in the wind, heat up, burn out. My father and I

never considered how far our lights might shine
when our fingers were bone-numb, braiding bulbs

into the cedar trees stiff with frost.
Only get them up while his good temper lasted,

as undependable as the weather in December.
His sudden anger, and slamming doors on life

with us to blame, followed by a terrible night
sky silence that made our mother feel small –

all this in hiding, while going inside to warm up,
and untangle more lights to string on a tree

trying to settle its branches in our house.
Now, years later, I twine lights up

the trunk of a tree so big it commands the room
and the spirits of our children. My body between the wall

and the tree, in the smell of its balsam wildness.
I still hear his voice circling impatience,

feel the silence piled up inside me
like the snow that stays. Once a year,

his effort to be jolly, bright as the stars we love
to watch burn holes in the cold and darkness.

The Witness

I walk my son and his friend by the painted rocks and broken glass
to the old burnt-down house, with its charred roof touching the
floor the way adults sometimes reach for their toes. We see pieces of
table and chair, bedposts rusty as anchors. The boys lean over the
concrete foundation, dropping rocks into timbers stacked like a
game of burnt-over pick-up sticks. His friend wonders what hap-
pened to the TV. 'Too dirty here. They probably took it away.' My
son looks into the sky. 'No power lines,' he says, 'there was never a
TV here.' We walk home along the railway tracks, by yellow coltsfoot
pushing through stones, by the willows wearing new green, subtle
as the ocean heard inland.

Crocuses

Crocuses are the earth's first dream in colour towards morning. Years ago they broke for me a long winter in Amsterdam. That spring we lost scarves in the streets, followed the hurdy-gurdy man, watched strangers look at themselves in a new city. I forgot the damp nights on a houseboat, the only art looking out a window holding the canal and the cold world still for awhile. The man I didn't love pedalling his bicycle into the fog with such finality and grace, I grieved; best move he made all winter. That summer I travelled over the dykes holding back the North Sea. Claiming land so new, the wild peacocks and storks moved in before the mapmakers arrived with their coloured pens and bags of place names. Twenty years later in my backyard garden, the crocuses bloom the colours of water rethinking itself. I love the way they stay closed on a cloudy day. Alert, knowing the rain comes.

Dishwasher

Our old dishwasher sits in the driveway. For years it churned dirt and dishes, jabbered at cutlery, in our tiny kitchen. I'd lie in bed, sure it was burning a hole in the floor and ceiling before blast-off into the pitiless winter sky. To hurtle down light-years to a planet where upright creatures still nibbled food off sticks and flat stones.

Now our children take it apart, bit by strip by chunk, with their father's tools. Friends arrive. They push it over, tap all its compass points, sing inside it. At the end of the day, washers and screws, red plastic popsicle sticks, a pump and tubes, old gum, the dishwasher's door, the motor, strips of trim, chrome buttons, bouquets of variegated wires, screwdrivers, the aluminium spinner, socks, and foreign metal parts litter our driveway. When the metal pounding stops, I look out the window. I see two children coast to the end of the driveway in the wheeled bottom dishrack. Hands gripping the rim for the right-angle turn to the sidewalk. Shifting their weight to steer around the concrete heaves and cracks, for one wild ride to the bottom of the hill.

First Day of School

The morning my daughter tossed the
hydrangea flowers on the kitchen counter
was the fall she started school. For days
I poured tea, spread butter, peeled onions
around that soft white mound of fading pink,
heaped careless as her clothes on the bedroom floor.
Petals curled like old papers and my husband
grumbled at the space her flowers claimed.
But for me, they filled what was left,
after we walked her over the hill,
came home, my son and I,
to the rose bush
bruised with hips
so red, I had to
look for boats
pulling wakes out the harbour
to sea.

There Are Two Stills

One
of her sitting
with bowed head
beside his bed
holding the blue
tipped reptilian hand.

The other
on a lake in early spring
carrying what is left
in a cardboard box
in a cedar canoe.

To my surprise
the fine ash sinks
        slowly,
ignites fierce
        silver rain
like fireworks
feeding the night.

The Onion Mountains

At the foot of the mountain, we found the trail followed
by so many before us. Angling up to the scent of onions
growing wild as the rocks. We'd been warned of the passes
never the same, the storms praising darkness,
the ledges no more than granite funnels
for the wind and our bodies. What vegetation
grew up there was wrung by the hands
of something I never saw, except
for the stubborn onions stinging our eyes,
bruising our lungs. We tried to stay sure
as the old bear following the scent of water,
knowing fire burns behind him. But even the strongest
among us lay down often. And when we stopped again,
our heads swollen, ears ringing from the bells
we heard swing deep in the cliffs, someone cursed the rocks
and their stinking crop. Which is why, at the ravine's edge,
I said, why blame the onions? We've climbed into air
meant only for the birds to spread their wings on.

  Little-bug-in-the-breeze, they called me,
do you know how far your voice travels up here?
Your words might anger the sun wearing clouds
so it too won't lose its way in these mountains.

They sent me ahead to gather wild onions
to sell in the villages still some five days away
and below us. And when we descended,
leaving the dull foothills behind, the sun appeared,
and the dogs ignored us to bark at the light.

Once I Followed a Bird Without a Heart

Once I followed a bird without a heart.

It circled the marsh
and I heard rhythm
in the lily pad leaves.

Always in the leaves,
the way they shudder
before the rain comes.

Once I followed a bird without a heart.

I found a white
tipped wing floating
in the lake.

I called the wing mine,
and the sound of rain
fell from my hands.

I followed my bird without a heart

to a tree
where a man played his violin.

A trail of sound
over a field of wet grass.

My bird loved him and stayed.

When the foliage is gone
I listen for the singing
in the trees.

And when the leaves come
I will watch them tremble,
the hearts of birds beating.

After the Storm

On the day after the night our boats
filled up with rain, all the insects
of the world burst into flames, lit
the holes that were once our eyes,
and last we saw was the wind
pulling fire down the valley, out to sea.
All that year we waited for sightings,
any verification of blazing tails
offshore. But even boats the waves favoured
never returned, became the memory
of birds singing for dawn. Now our nights
are so black, even windows are lost,
sleep too private, too long.

An Ancient Child

The doctor's waiting room, the quiet flip
of magazine pages. My daughter's right lung
still crackling, and I wish for recovery
and punctual doctors. Looking at the floral patterns
of china I'll never buy, when suddenly my daughter laughs,
holds up for me to see spread across
two pages, a photo of a black child left to die
    where it fell. White eyes,
canyon cheeks, protruding teeth. She sees

my shock and says, 'The face is funny.
Like something from Halloween.'

I look again, the image so intimate,
if I lean too close I'll smell decay.
Hear wind rattle the shacks left standing,
feel a foreign sun's heat baking
the skin draped over a small skeleton.

An ancient child feeding birds and insects
    and photographer's lenses. If only

I could reach in, feel the rubber
moulded into a face falling in on itself
like an old grave. Find the edge of the mask
my daughter saw and peel it off.
    Expose the child smiling
underneath, waiting to say,
    'See, I tricked you.'

Hartlen Point

As I pick up what the hurricane tore off our trees,
I think of the drive to see the storm's surf
        pound Hartlen Point last night.
How my son and I watched our friends trudge
into the wind and rain that shook our car
in the darkness. A circus ride he
wanted to stop and get off. Go home.

We talked of dinosaurs as big as this storm,
and the comet we saw last spring, just left
of the Big Dipper's handle. Out here, away
from city lights, the reluctant fingerprint
of a traveller not wanting company. My son
wondered where the comet could be now, how far
        it might go before it collides
with a ringed planet. I thought how close
it came to never entering our sight at all.

Now I store winter kindling, curse the cat
who brought home the cedar waxwing.
The bird who survived last night's storm
        tossed broken on our driveway.
The body ripped open, the pavement
stained with blood bright as red currants,
        place names on a map.

Premonition

You tie the canoe to a tree, climb a slope,
find an old road left alone,
its grass and clover humming

to the foliage so persuasive above.
A road once graded for cars
trailing dust, leaving the

city behind. Now a lane
tangled as your hair in the morning,
direction growing over.

You admire the purple vetch
gripping tall plumed grasses
under a sumac

thinking red for fall.
It's there you see yourself
as an old woman,

sowing a wild garden
beyond the rotten planks
in the bridge

still crossing the creek.

Smudgeling

Oh stealthy hunter of bugs
in the red poppy jungle,
I loved when the blue jay

screeched in the tree
above you, 'run, run,
the fire-dogs come!'

Your streak for cover,
outwitting ambush,
cheetah-swift.

Fiction

It's the nun looking for a lost dog in the pictures of my daughter's book that reminds me. When I was six years old, a nun lived at the end of our street, close to the sawdust pile where we played. Her house was white and as big as ours. Only the trees, tall enough to look in windows, knew anything about her. She never sat on her porch or turned earth in her garden, no man ever cleared snow from her driveway. I saw her once, the back of her coat tea-leaf brown and thin, compared to my mother's shiny sealskin. One afternoon we made a mess of snow angels all over her yard. Ran away, leaving the Virgin Mary in her backyard grotto, to watch the snow fall on what we'd done. A few days later I found a small New Testament lying in the slush close to her house. I thought it was a sign left by the nun, telling us she knew of our angels buried in the snow. A detour made by a woman who, while our mothers made dinners and ironed clothes, prayed in a quiet room without moving her lips. Not like this nun on the page, who searches through the park's spring green on a cloudy day, her voice as loud as the children's, calling for the lost dog.

For My Feet, Still in Shoes

When he picks up his fiddle, all the bears at home in the flannelette gray hills listen. The wind starts to move the stars around and the backs of frogs gleam bright as tin cans under a full moon. The way tails chase cats, that's how the sound knows where to go. Wild enough to blow the numbers right out of those digital clocks that run our lives. When he plays, the crickets remember they've seen water run uphill, rise in the air like a snake charmed silver with sound. There's nothing left for the wind's eye to find when he stops, no echo from the bedrock cold below. Only the bears licking clean their dragonfly wings. And my feet, still in shoes, but restless as stones polished by the bellies of fish on urgent journeys.

Mr. Philips

Some days, down the wooden stairs to the basement, to sit in rows in a room with chain-link fencing over the windows. Ready to watch a bony man with a quartz-white face and hands teach us music. In his British accent, dusting chalk off his fingers, tapping the music stand with a yellow-tipped pointer. Some notes black and solid, others letting the page shine through their holes. Folding pink sheets of bubblegum into our mouths and sorting Beatles cards, we made fun of this man who separated girls from boys for the sake of voice. We couldn't imagine his life outside that room, for we knew he slept there in his black suit and tie, head pillowed on sheet music, listening. When we returned to school after Christmas, they told us he'd died from pneumonia over the holidays. For awhile we wondered if he'd been dying at the front of that room, all those times he insisted we sing together underground. By spring we'd forgotten him, singing our own songs, skipping rope or clapping hands.

Years later I draw treble clefs in phonebook margins while waiting for someone to answer my call. 'Will you hold?' she asks from the other end of the line, and the receiver makes music for me. It's then I think of him, wonder how he found passage through the long days in that mill town on the river. What he knew, but couldn't pass on, even if we had wanted to listen.

For the Man Playing His Charango

One afternoon
I sat down by the harbour
to watch a man play his charango.

The water lay still in the heat,
and my heart was the boat not taken,
    tied up to a tree.

His fingers sure on ten strings
stretched over a dried armadillo shell.

I heard water leave the ground,
    snow fall on flowers high in the mountains,
a small animal running for cover.

His face grave as stone on the ground unturned.
And dark, and in the cool evening
his thick hair hung down his back to his waist,

    black water falling over a ledge.

Lord, if You Had a Lap

Lord, if you had a lap, I'd sit on it tonight.
I'd tell you how my hurting songs have come true
at last. My speaking voice stuck
as my singing sounds on those 2,000
newly pressed records from Toronto.
Every single one of them skipping
to repeat my lines, sure as Lela Bennett's
dog's tail used to thump the kitchen floor
when I walked in her back door
for beer and sweet rolls. Lord, hear my voice,
broken as the next shipment of records
I poured like cornflakes from boxes
marked 'fragile'. To get away, Lela and I
rode the Yarmouth-Bar-Harbour ferry in March,
rode a storm that drove all those big truck drivers
out of the lounge, their hands held over their mouths
to catch their insides boiling over. Just me
and Lela left to share fried smelts and potatoes,
watch the curtains swing as if that gale roared
through the dining room. And every time that boat reared
then fell, to meet the ocean,
her metal buzzed like an out-of-tune loose string
on my guitar. You heard me then, Lord,
thanking you for boats that stay upright,
good food and patience. It took them two hours
to chip the ice from the ferry doors
so we could drive my old Ford Fairlane south
under trees wearing flowers all pink and white
and brighter than any sequinned shirt I ever wore.

It's there I told Lela she carried for me
more melody than I could ever write.
I thought she heard me then and I thought
she heard me since, but this spring back home
she found a man loving his saxophone
and her watching him while he plays bars
with a back-up band spinning tunes
I couldn't copy if I tried.

Leaving me to write new songs
on a pile of empties growing fast
as the good lines keep coming.
Lord, could I pop you a beer to celebrate
those 2,000 broken records remade
into tapes small enough to navigate this world's
great fickle current before freeze-up.
But Lord, will anyone hear me this time?

Five Islands

When words gather for the long journey to water,
dust coats my tongue. Even highrise-building lights
filling the dusk, read like lines
            escaping prose.

Haze rests on the silver harbour, and I've lost
the line demanding ocean give sky some space.
What would grow if I threw seed
into the furrow dragged by a small boat
            heading inland?

            Once on a hill in spring
I saw five islands float in the Bay of Fundy,
all parts alive in the trees
growing up or stunted through seasons,
the rock knowing when to let go for saltwater. A poem,
even when fog hides the coastline, the ocean, the sky.

Briefly, Abelard Tries to Understand

Abelard, the cat, who's been
around, would have his friend, Manon, believe
that life is God inhaling, and that death
comes when God's nostrils are empty. She says, Abelard,
why do you keep hunting with the neighbourhood cats?
They fight over leftovers and brag of feasts.
Who do you know besides bully racoons, a few skunks,
and rats? He murmurs, life could be short
if God becomes asthmatic. Besides,
what else is there to do?
She cleans an umber-coloured paw, and says,
one day I swam out to the islands
at the harbour's mouth where seals watch land
that never floats away. The water so foreign,
and willing to feed me to the red-eyed fish
circling below. Court a bird, make it your friend.
Or carry a mouse still warm to the coyote
who claims the unlit alley behind the restaurant.
See if he thanks you. She lies down under ferns
curling from the ground, and he remembers the time
she insisted he listen to the red poppies
pull their petals in at dusk. All he'd heard was the ocean
grieving for something he didn't understand, eyed the crow
in the tree for the contents of its shiny belly.

Manchurian Evening

I

In the long Manchurian evening, she remembers the women
burying crosses in hills west of the village.
How the tiger came down from the mountains to walk with children.
A corner of her garden grows in winter, she tends it
like a cautious lover. On her clothes,
on her pillow cases, she embroiders black peonies.
No one sits with her now, no one listens to her stories.
She eats bread in the early twilight,
watches ice thicken on the inside of her window.
When she was young, under a trellis of melons and beans, her father
had warned her, only tell stories of wolves in the winter.
Tell them out of season, and you'll change the weather.

II

In the long Manchurian evening, a man sharpens
his knife, hears the highway bypass his town.
He is not a hunter like his father. He counts hours
in the bottle factory, watches the woman who lost
a breast. Story or memory, like a monkey
on a leash, leads him on. One evening when a boy
he leaned into a well, listening. Back then
streams flowed by night, not by day.
He turned to the heat on his neck, saw the tiger,
eyes wilder than anything his father carried home.
Now he longs for the shortest day of the year.
He will build a fire in the middle of the frozen lake,
    sit and listen, how the ice holds heat.

III

In the long Manchurian afternoon, a child
rubs her eyes, asks for a story. Her grandmother
buried by the silty river with pearls in her mouth.
How a wild cat led her father when a boy through the snow
to the door of his house. The leaves of some trees
hang on in winter, they cannot stop listening,
she understands this. Her mother shuns the woman
who tells the child of a giant bell
buried in the hills. The girl paints
her face like her mother, wonders who to believe.
The crow she loves to watch fly through
all kinds of weather, does he land on a bell exposed
by the wind, by wolves digging the earth for homes?

The Voice That Trails You

The voice that trails your waking at night
could be your child walking a railway bridge
inside her dream. Calling you because
she sees the train come. Or do you hear
the back door swing open, your mother
luring you home years ago when the streetlights
flickered on. Or a lover whispering your name
to himself, wanting to know the origins of sound
by repeating your name. Maybe a siren
dying before the only house on a side street
is all you hear. A cry that trails
you leaving sleep, as a hawk follows trees
    edging an old logging road.

What Stopped Me

I closed Tolstoy's *War and Peace*, left behind
old Russia and our cabin full of kids, and the adults
more comfortable with Merle Haggard's troubles
than their own. Entered the rain and darkness
tied to a flashlight's beam. Trusting the light
to find puddles in a storm among trees
hinting of a night life foreign to us.

Call it my life trailing fiction, or the pressure
of silence after noise. What stopped me
was the face on the outhouse door. A face
I'd never seen before, protruding from boards
above the handle, just below the window.
A jowled, old-man's face, his copper-
kettle eyes looking at me.
                            Because I trust reflections,
the mirrored lightning on a lake making me look up,
I stayed. In the rain with my light, the water
finding the seams of my coat at last, always
the good listener, I stayed.

He offered no warnings or prophecies. Just a moment
of quiet collision. *It's hard to fish in the dark,*
he said. Voice intimate as the radio
turned down low. A pause, then,
Even duct tape can't mend a broken heart,
        his face and voice
fading on *heart*. Left me staring
at the door's chewed bug trails
and knot holes, odd map to nowhere.

Often I've wondered why me and why that door?
The mistake is to tell anybody, look what happened
at Lourdes and Fatima, spoiled
the places forever, too many people begging
for a slice of miracle on the spot. Of course
it's an act of faith to fish anytime, especially
without sonar, and some men I know would say
             only a year-long fishing trip
             can patch a hole in a heart.
                                    Now I think
that face a gift of private song. I never doubted
my sight or my hand holding the flashlight.
I keep thinking of the immense, full life
in *War and Peace*, how Tolstoy describes
guests, 'congregated like rye shaken together
in a shovel.' They don't know I watch them,
they don't know Tolstoy would rewrite
some passages if he had a chance. These days
even the shower curtains have potential,
could speak to me at any time. Last summer's
razor clam shell on my desk, it too
informed by volumes of sand and ocean
could sing at any moment, in a tongue
I might not understand.

Scissors

Tonight I'll take my scissors to the movies. When everyone has surrendered to the screen, like starfish splayed under the sun, I'll sneak up to those landscapes and cut out passages. Of Babette setting her stuffed quail on the table, the child hidden in the house on the ashen moors. Clip stills of the severed finger, the lover still breathing on the tattered boat, the porpoise come home again. I'll set these urgencies loose on my street, for I have failed to see anymore the same kleptomaniac, the same quilter and potholes, the same peonies as last year dropping their petals. Carrying home groceries, I'll be the first to tell a neighbour of the concubine's slipper left in the grass. Be the only witness to the killer tomato eating the Dicky-Dee boy, bells and all. Tell my husband, over dinner, of the cowboy who put down his pistols in the late afternoon sun by the laundromat and followed me home. But the holes my scissors leave behind are big enough to fall into. Something informs them, asks me, like my son did the other day, what is it our souls help us to do? I think about this as my daughter carries what's left of her meal to the fugitive she's hiding in the garage. In a few years she'll write us sad letters from a shack in the swamps where he's fixing outboard motors and hunting snakes. I turn on the TV, slide in a cassette. Surely a small screen will be safer to watch, impossible to carry away in pieces.

The Man in Blue

The man in blue lives on my yellow mug.
He carries a spade over his shoulder, and a basket
of greens on his arm while he walks to market,
or home around the base of my mug. Under the sun
and the ivory mountains, by the elephant ear tree
nearly touching the sky. While I sleep, he walks,
his pipe trailing smoke over his hat, the sun
heating his world and my winter cupboard. My morning mug
warms my hands, smells of crushed leaves and tobacco,
before I fill it with coffee. Does he listen when I stir
the heat with a metal spoon that warms up too?
Does he know I look out my window to trees struck dumb
with ice? To watch a woman under her black umbrella
feed bread to the ducks in the freezing rain.

For Snow

Walking by the old canal, I see frost glitter
on the coffee-brown back of a mallard duck
treading slow circles in water still flowing
between banks of new ice. I think of the duck
slicing its webbed feet on this first ice
pushing jagged and bright as new teeth
through the cut stone dislodged. I walk the body
of grass, its matted yellow stiff
under sky, indifferent beyond windows.
It breaks bones, this ground, it should lie
under days and nights of white release.
Hear the wind speaking in drifts
and the children
carving tunnels of blue light.

Admitting Winter

Tonight my heart is a stone wrapped in cloth.
I wonder about yours, you by the river in the cabin
without me. Could it be like this fire I watch,
an intricate heat transforming a tree once whole
and hanging on to what's left of its colour
in the fall? The leaves so brilliant, they force the light
of their dreams before dying through our windows, into our rooms
as the nights grow longer. Soon the sound of those leaves
will be gone. And our bodies, described by the rustle
of our hands under old blankets, pushing away shadows
to find a pulse waiting all these years to quicken,
to throw light on the snow falling outside.

Down the Bow

This morning I'll go down to the Bow River
to wash my hands. In water I hear ripple
by the ice that still holds prints from the elk
and silver fox it supported last night.
With my clean hands, I'll carry away
the child that died inside you.

And the guilt you feel, I'll take that too.
Float it down the Bow, past the woodpecker
impregnating silence with hunger.
Into the mountains, where the measured breathing
of hibernating bears warms their hidden dens.
Guilt's heartbeat slows down too,
grows tired, sleeps awhile.

But I think sorrow is the bird
we must feed so it can fly away.
Throw food on top of the snow.
And when it returns, hungry again,
watch how this bird opens seeds,
the pattern of broken shells
it leaves on a crust
frozen to stay. Learn to listen
to its song.

The Cherry Tree

A distant train reminds me of other journeys
I've taken. A whistle pulling me towards
a family stunned by death's abrupt arrival.
And once, my daughter and I, through dark hills
pulsing with fireflies and heat lightning,
her brother beginning to fill my belly. Now
the applause of rain on leaves adds up our days.
Eases off, a tip-tapping, bountiful murmur.
When it stops, the neighbourhood kids
and blue jays come to strip our tree of cherries.
Sudden ammunition, how to spit a pit at a friend.
Wings flapping, raucous squawking, over the fruit
and green leafage. Who can argue with sequence?
White blossoms, then the cherries, now these appetites.

Before the Phoenicians

Last night we lay under the stars with a map
and a flashlight, the lake beside us
reflecting passages we found in the sky.
Named by the Phoenicians – Draco the dragon,
the Dippers, and the shifting pole star, Thuban,
the pyramid builders used to orient their stones.
And someone said the fires we see up there
could be the light still travelling from stars
dead for thousands of years, finding our eyes only now.

I feel closer to the dead ones floating on the creek
       I paddle on this morning.
Those fallen stars that wake up as water lilies,
the chosen ones, their afterlives burning white
in this dark pool. Such poise
after their long fall and burnout.
       For the damselflies
       and choirs of frogs they bloom,
       they live in the tiny currents
       spun by the sunfish and perch swimming below.

And I am here before the Phoenicians,
drifting among these fallen stars
that do not play tricks on me with time and light.
I find no constellations here,
do not whisper names to the white fires.
I follow the kingfisher downstream
to the lake where the lilies don't grow.

When You Can't Leave Me Anymore

The day you fly to Tennessee, the snow
begins to fall. April snow berating the crocuses
and tulips, falling as if it cannot stand
for another minute the ground warming up
in early spring. At dusk, our children go out to play.
They build a snowman, work together in a wind
that rearranges our backyard. He props up the head
while she punches in a carrot-nose.
Pulls off his mittens to press popsicle sticks
into a v-shaped grin. She finds pebble eyes
and tree-branch arms spread wide.

I watch them play so I can tell you
when you come home how the bodies we made
are still close in their short time together.
I think of death, when spring storms will rage on
without me, when you can't leave me anymore.
My memories of you and them broken
like those flakes filling the air.
Pieces of me and what I remember
carried off in my children and you
going places I won't know.

Songs for Marion's Daughter

Marion

(1862–1948)

She comes from Boundary Creek, where the ships are stopped by the river's muddy banks converging. A brown, salt-water river receiving the creek, and the runs of smelt and salmon. She marries Henry, whose father sailed ships on the tides that fed the currents so sly he never saw them, only felt their tug all the way down the river to the Bay of Fundy and beyond. They settle in nearby Salisbury, where barrels of oats and fish and flour, cords of lumber change hands everyday at the train station. Where Henry goes to pick up supplies for his General Store. On the platform, a woman offers passengers all the eggs boiled black in her teapot. And around the corner, Marion rolls oatcakes in a small house not far from the wooden bridge that carries the road across the river.

Spring

She watches winter reluctant to leave,
how April snow tries to douse the flames of new buds.
More ice laces the edges of the puddles
on a road so plugged with mud, she lifts her skirts
to reach the wooden sidewalk, the doctor's house.
Does her confession of weariness, the dry well
that grows deeper at night,
does it come before or after the death
of her first child, her son, only ten months old?

The doctor tells her to get out of the house
more often. When she goes home, he leaves
his office, walks through the mud to the General Store
to look for Henry. He says, 'Henry,
listen to me. There's two kinds of horses.
Do you know what they are?
Some horses, they're work horses.
Others are dainty fillies.

Your wife, now she's a dainty filly.'

Getting Out

On her bicycle, she leaves the village
for the fields of cows with nothing better to do
than lie down or stand up to eat.
Down the road, dusty, pocked with ruts,
the clank of metal when she hits a stone,
quick intake of breath as she bounces over
to land upright. By the clover sweet as a child
on its way, the goldenrod so bright she knows
why crickets have to sing. She pedals past farms
to the woods, her legs stretching like the currents
she's seen work the river. Does she turn for home at last
with a sigh, this morning's sour milk still coating
her tongue? Or, with wit restored, and spreadable
as new sweet butter, over
his complaints of work not done.

Trying to Sleep

There comes a time she can't sleep at night.
She goes back to the doctor who knows so much
about horses. He gives her sleeping pills,
to close her eyes, to lose herself in dreams,
the only colour cinema available back then.

Later that day he leaves the tavern, waves to her
across the street, roars, 'My oh my – will you
ever sleep tonight!' Like a deer startled by smoke,
she strides up the cedar lined driveway to their new house,
pours all those pills down Salisbury's first indoor toilet.

Asking for Money

She dumps flour into a bowl, cuts
in the shortening, asks Henry,
'How much change do you
have in your pocket?'

Puts down his book, reaches into
his pocket, jiggles coins
in his hand, 'This much.'

'How much?'

Extends his arm, the coins
in the flat of his hand,
'This much.'

She moves closer,
'Let's see.'

Quick
as cracking an egg one-handed
she swats his palm up
shoots the coins
straight into the air

       to the floor
       with little drumrolls.
       Clatter, lie still.

She pats out
the biscuit dough.
'Don't have any now, do you?'

He sighs, stoops
to hide his smile, begins
to pick up
the nickels
the dimes

just like
the last time she asked
him for change.

The Yellow Bird

An injured wing. That's what Marion says of the bird lying in her daughter's hand. Its feathers brighter than the petals of a sunflower. She does not suggest giving it back to the cat as Henry does when he comes home to eat. He strokes the egg-yolk coloured body. 'A bird minus a wing is no bird at all,' he says. The bird lives to walk over pies ready for the oven, to eat dandelion seeds from the girl's hand. To land on curtain rods, the backs of chairs, the top of Henry's shiny head. In the fall, the girl called Helen leaves the house with the bird perched on her finger, walks to the General Store, walks slow as clouds gathering on the surface of a lake. She wants to show her father how stillness works for her, how a bird will choose to rest on her finger because she does not order it to. The girl and the bird on the dusty road, the world stretching big and quiet around them, that's what she remembers.

The Daughter

(1895–1983)

Helen grows up in the new house to climb, with a book,
the russet apple tree out back. She wades
the creek in summer, waits with her two brothers
for winter's crusty, fast rendition of that long hill
pulling away from the village. The scraped knees,
the hands, raw as radishes from the hard snow.
She's sent to the farm to fetch milk,
to the back shed for headcheese prickled with frost,
they slice with Friday night's baked beans.
Once a week with friends she waits for the train
to see who gets off, who climbs on to know
the heat and storms of other places. Hillsborough,
Moncton, Sussex, Saint John. Other places.

In her eleventh summer
she walks a log across the creek,
looks back to see her older brother
fall off with petit mal grace
into water that finds his lungs
faster than she can reach him.
     Left with a shell of a brother
         left
     while the other runs for help,
    for Marion.

On the Train

For Helen, the journey is not complete without bridges
and their possibilities. Imagine the train falling
when the trestle breaks over the Shepody River
like it did three years before she was born.
The crew and seven passengers living to tell the tale,
including a woman who claims she was guided from the coach
by her lately departed husband's ghost calling to her
from the salt grasses. Now Helen watches trees deep as water
flow by her window, a picture on a page she never has to turn.
This train carries her and her mother and brother
to where the brown river muscles the mud banks
far apart, the river sensing something bigger
than itself. They are met by family at Hillsborough
for a short vacation, the air cooler here.
Helen watches the train pull away
towards the bridge she knows they never rebuilt.
Tore up the tracks, leaving coastal villages like Alma,
with its low-tide glistening beach, alone
on a trail they called a road. Like her mother,
so quiet since they carried the dead boy home,
stalled on a private road neither can name
or find on a map.

In the Cards

Helen turns down the Baptist preacher
who proposes to her in a row boat under a full moon.
She leaves with Tommy for Newfoundland
to live in a city built on rock, the fog
a frequent visitor. She calls it home,
has four children, and they live their summers
beside a river in a canvas tent, her daughter's
salmon hauled in by hand on a broken line,
the polished water tugging at her feet.

From Salisbury, Marion writes that an untended wood stove
and a late afternoon card game in the back room
sent Henry's General Store up in flames.
When Helen writes home, she does not mention
her weekly excursions, even when ill with pregnancy.
Last night, leaning over the front porch railing
to throw up in the neighbour's peonies, then taking
Tommy's arm, feeling strong enough to enter
the house for the next round of poker with friends.

Departures

On one of their visits, Henry complains
of stomach cramps, resents the pain, out comes
the bottle of castor oil. Marion pours,
and he accepts the spoonfuls with the faith of a child.
She pours with experience, knows that nothing else
in the house can purge the overworked stomach and bowels.
The pain cries louder than Henry, he curls up like a fist.

The surgeon tells her that castor oil
was the worst thing she could have given
to a man with ulcers like he'd suffered. They bury
him far away from the large stone in Salisbury
that marks where the earth covers
their sons. The stone
with the space left on it to receive his name
and hers. Six years later, she lies down
beside him, in Newfoundland, a foreign land back then.

These Stories

When I grew strong enough to carry what I needed
on my back, I followed roads nearly grown over
along the Bay of Fundy. Or the animal trails
through its forests, delicate paths
as hard to see as the currents
out there in the muddy bay. I camped for days
in a cove, searching for fiddleheads
curled up and listening in the hills. The surprise
of a crow flying over the beach to the cliffs
with my last loaf of bread. The tide claiming rocks
I'd climbed on earlier. And always I carried those stories
passed down by Helen, my grandmother,

with me. These stories informed by days of chores,
the tea poured and the need to give away something
more distilled than wine or the berries crushed
and preserved in jars. A rug thwacking the wind
and the eyes of the woman watching it. The days
pared down, all pain and loss kneaded like bread dough
into something that keeps growing, that feeds more
than my stomach.

Sometimes I think the stories the dead
take with them live on like bats
away from light. These stories I sense
at night as dark and swift, so sure of themselves
they no longer need to collide with memories
that fail us. My grandmother, before she died,
calling for her mother, for Marion,
calling, and surprised when I told her
Marion had been gone for thirty-five years.

Acknowledgements

Thanks to the editors of the following publications, where some of these poems first appeared: *The Fiddlehead, TickleAce, Pottersfield Portfolio, Grain, Antigonish Review, The Amethyst Review, Canadian Author, Contemporary Verse,* and *Zygote.* And also to the editors of *Windhorse Reader* and *Anthology of Magazine Verse and Yearbook of American Poetry* for reprinting some of them.

Thanks to friends and fellow writers who listened and gave feedback, especially to members of the Halifax Poetry Workshop. Also to Don McKay and Robert Hilles at the Banff Centre for the Arts. Special thanks to the folks at the Writers' Federation of Nova Scotia and to my editor, John Donlan. I am grateful to Jan Zwicky for her years of patient listening and for giving me encouragement when I most needed it. And to John McConnell, who helps me find the time and the place to write.

'Manchurian Evening' is indebted to Jung Chang's *Wild Swans.*

'Lord, if You Had a Lap' was inspired by a story on country and western singer, Laurie Spears, printed in the *Dartmouth Patriot,* December, 1992.

'The Flamingo' was the winner of the Lina Chartrand Award in 1995.

The translator of the quotation from Machado is Robert Bly.

'Down the Bow' is for Kim Kieran. 'When a Child Gets Lost' is for Sue Goyette. 'Dishwasher' is for all the kids who played on Harbour Drive in the spring of 1996.

Lynn's non-fiction has appeared in many Canadian magazines, her stories for children have been published in various anthologies. After a 16 year sojourn in Nova Scotia, Lynn now lives with her family on McLeod Hill, New Brunswick. *The Bridge That Carries the Road* is her first book.